PRAISE FOR *CITY OF DIS*

Reginald Shepherd called us out twenty years ago: we're all urban now, but we've been stuck in a rural poetics, "still struggling toward a poetic language of the city." Until now. Randall Tyrone just invented that language. Tyrone's city is mythical and abyssal and oracular and real. It is where we live, and who we are. *City of Dis* is not a place of "my heart with pleasure fills, / And dances with the daffodils"; it is a place of "Tell me pushpin cubical tapestry / who do I work for," packed here "like gunpowder / in a suicidal chamber." Welcome to the City of Dis. We're not in the Lake District anymore.

—**H. L. HIX,** AUTHOR OF *AMERICAN OUTRAGE*

Tyrone's *City of Dis* interrupts the conversation about what a poem should do, about what a poem is capable of today, if anything at all. With urgency and the courage to experiment with the tradition and make his moment wholly his own, Tyrone makes you stand up and take inventory of what you've done and hold yourself accountable for forgetting what poetry can do.

—**JOSHUA ROBBINS,** AUTHOR OF *ESCHATOLOGY IN CRAYON WAX*

CITY OF DIS

CITY OF DIS

RANDALL JAMES TYRONE

Poems

TRP: The University Press of SHSU
Huntsville, Texas 77341

Library of Congress Cataloging-in-Publication Data

Names: Tyrone, Randall James, 1990- author.
Title: City of Dis : poems / Randall James Tyrone.
Description: First edition. | Huntsville, Texas : TRP: The University Press of SHSU, [2025]
Identifiers: LCCN 2025018754 (print) | LCCN 2025018755 (ebook) | ISBN 9781680034325 (trade paperback) | ISBN 9781680034332 (ebook)
Subjects: LCSH: Street life--United States--Poetry. | LCGFT: Poetry.
Classification: LCC PS3620.Y76 C58 2025 (print) | LCC PS3620.Y76 (ebook) | DDC 811/.6--dc23/eng/20250422
LC record available at https://lccn.loc.gov/2025018754
LC ebook record available at https://lccn.loc.gov/2025018755

FIRST EDITION

Cover art by FYHA Clothing Co.
Author photo by Ramelle Ramos

Cover design by Cody Gates, Happenstance Type-O-Rama
Interior design by Maureen Forys, Happenstance Type-O-Rama

Printed and bound in the United States of America
First Edition Copyright: 2025

TRP: The University Press of SHSU
Huntsville, Texas 77341
texasreviewpress.org

For Uncle Paul,

Uncle Sack, and

Pops/Mark,

I'm sorry I took too long

CONTENTS

BODY

SPIRIT

GHOST WEARING A DEAD GUY

THE BODY

SUNFLOWERS

Sometimes

sometimes   sunflowers grow out of the concrete

Sometimes

sometimes   they grow about a one & two thirds' miles high

Towering

Towering   over lawns over houses
over projects & over neighbors alike

Sometimes

sometimes   at the top   with enough luck   God sometimes

sometimes   stops to answer the hard questions

My Mom   elementary school young
climbed one once to meet God
Sitting on furniture built out of holiday bullets
fired into the sky they debated
what the other should want

My Mom asked *Will I have a future*
God said *The past is all that is real*
it has happened
The future I cannot speak
Then God lost their voice

My Mom asked *Why did the firefighters let my classmate burn*
to death in that car wreck
God looked down at the City

through the clouds   to the parts outside the garden
Looked past the white men in heat reflective armor
past their jovial talk
to the black girl trapped in a melting cage
Burning brighter & brighter & brighter
& brighter still   Then God lost their sight

My Mom asked *Is life hard for you*
God revealed the crucifixion marks
on their heart Three smokestacks blocking three valves
& a testing warhead in the side
Then God lost their mind

In the fantastical   whimsy can turn to horror
faster than the passing of time between heartbeats

Sometimes

sometimes

in this City   the one with sunflower skyscrapers
                      the one where my Mom climbed down one
                      to escape God   we still pray

SURVEILLANCE   A DAY IN THE CITY

i love staring at the billboards'
flashing cartoon commercials
They feel like Tylenol
when the lights are too hard
After the wild coyote falls
off a cliff there's a rainbow
with a new Tylenol to take
This one's for coughs
i take Tylenol every day now
Mom doesn't

Why

She points at this World's gray roof
& lightning flinches like my migrained brain
She's trying to help me
learn what it is to be made
a way   to be different
i want to know what more is above the clouds
There's no answer

i'm in the City's crowd
The language is quiet   the loose translation
is keep moving   pushing Yes
it may be bleak & yes you may burn
under the lamp post in these streets
but keep pushing
            Past the sloppily packed
in offices & shelter   half a mile high

Implication
be grateful
This is before you know
the coldness
of a body

missing

21 grams

This is what you know
Blaming the membranes
that keep us whole
The cell wall banging of a brain
imprisoned in a skull
trying even eye sockets to escape
being unable to balance anxious nerve fibers
& a blood filled thought
The pills will numb it Be content
Be in the torrential downpour
Breathe in the nauseating steam
of Main Street as wetness hits
broiling concrete Rain & daylight
i am not too young to ask
if i'm strong enough for darkness
just too young to fear it if i'm not
Be content

i just wanted to take it all in
The streets are all flooded
with plastic pill bottles floating
around the gutter before me
Like my father's last words before we left
It doesn't make more sense
the more you see Take it all in
like all those days i saw a ravaged man's tin cup
waiting between his bruise shaded nails
like a red light waiting on change
outside the Bank's skyscraper
& Mom would always lean into me
& whisper
It's rude to stare

A WALL OF LOCOMOTIVES

i can't imagine making it
in America without crime
my Mom lied
about where we lived
because   the City determines where you go
by where you are
                    Determines what you breathe
by where you live

                    The City is held together
                    by train tracks
working like stitches on a body On my side
of the sutures the funding has bad circulation

The train horns keep me awake at night
The blares & baritone rumblings
shake our home
shake my bones
shake right below the sternum to the heart
of everything Interwoven
                              to get a better school
or a grocery store you had to cross over to better
You had to cross the tracks
trains would rest on in the morning
Blocking my way out   no vibrato horns
just running engines & us trapped
turned into traffic
waiting for our turn to cheat

NAMING GAME

my Priest told me
that in the book of Genesis
humans are given the power to name
They named everything
from beast to plants
to the lights loitering in the sky

In the Principal's office   again
This Lord of Flapping Gums
Has once again been caught
naming his classmates
                One best friend forever
                Some enemies for naming me enemy
                Some beautiful   One too beautiful

my teacher has not been named
Yet Teacher has named me
& my Mom is called away
from her job   again

Named many things
i am mostly named U
                Unsatisfactory

In her room with a phone
Mom can be heard

            I don't know what to do
            with him

In my room with a used belt
with a bunk bed

Hard to breathe like suicide
Hard to grieve like suicide

HYSTERICAL

My neighbors are immortals or zombies   i guess i am too
& they necrotic shamble   & i can't say i don't   All my friends feel feral
or high or are arrested by white men in armor or black men that want to be
white men in armor or niggas that don't know what to be
or niggas indebted to lovers that know we ain't shit but need us to want more than a
want to be better
            i don't know how long we've been dead   buried under the cost of existence
the light   the water   the heat   Borrowing time   lease agreements line our graves
In my coffin   under my pillow   broken heart shaped teeth
i guess they're under every pillow   these offerings are everywhere

FROM THE MAILBOX BEATRICE SPEAKS

Tú

I was told about the Timelines broken down into missions. Are these people my brothers & sisters. How long will I blame myself when they die.

Beatrice
Pvt.

WHAT MORE DO YOU NEED FROM A LIFE BELOW THE SUN

My blinds are a dead wasp nest between me   & some squirrel
     climbing our tree in a spiral ascent   filled with morning
hunger The mail is piled up   My Mom's waiting   giving the news time to change
its mind   Be what she wants to see
The day has moved on without me   Before the locks are recommitted to keeping
the keyless out
i half-hear my Mom   on her way out the door
cry out   i'm lazy
           or
           goodbye   *i can't order my flesh to cooperate*

The paranoia of sadness   My Mom wouldn't call me lazy
just stand over the trash   i've not emptied   Stand in the squalor
my room has become   She is giving me time to change

                 but corpses rarely reanimate
             i decompose Simply letting my killer feast
                 & fatten like pecans for the squirrel
             out the window   preparing for a cold
                 that won't really come

           i can't order my flesh to cooperate

In the trash   written in letters   a Doctor's quote
           she'll be all bone & gristle
i can't make it out   the balled up pap smear results
findings of what's eating her

VICES WIND & COPPER

It's too hot to have the window closed
From beneath a tin roof veranda
out there I hear Virgil
Heard that mutha fucca bragging bout his
so let's see bout em
we gon see Dead bodies everywhere
most blood gets absorbed by the carpet in their dens
the rest rolls out in waves for help
Loitering in his complex stairwell
the shooter
a teething baby laughing

FROM THE MAILBOX BEATRICE SPEAKS

Tú

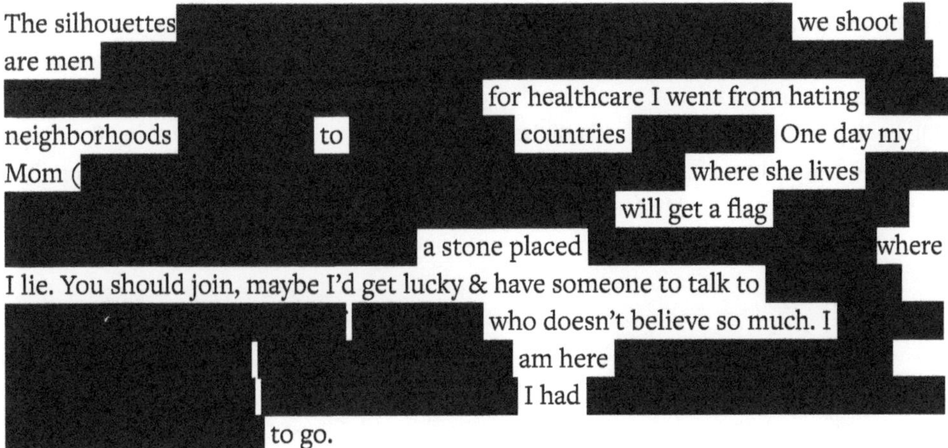
The silhouettes we shoot
are men
for healthcare I went from hating
neighborhoods to countries One day my
Mom (where she lives
will get a flag
a stone placed where
I lie. You should join, maybe I’d get lucky & have someone to talk to
who doesn’t believe so much. I
am here
I had
to go.

Beatrice
Pvt.

GLUTTONY

Sometimes the heat gets to you   Tim use to smell like a thirsty mouth full of
Cola   Sweating sugared water   he had that   *I don't know about you but I have*
holes I'm trying to fill   forehead strain   That   *I don't know about you but I have*
holes I have to feel lip quiver   i had hoped he'd get better   hoped he'd ignore the
gapping he sees in the mirror   stop using candy as patchwork   Yes   yes
losing his leg is the Sugar   is diabetic frostbite   He stopped eating & stopped
Just stopped   i saw him at a hundred pounds i see him roaming the halls when i'm
trying to sleep   My Mom doesn't know her son is a fool who expects to sleep
again

VICES   TONGUE DRIPPED

It's too hot   to have the window closed
Dante's voice   breaks into my open window
Aye   a Ma let me talk to you   Have you seen the sun
Aye   ain't we been baptized   why are we here   They talkin
they talkin   Can't you hear them   We all been washed but
but we still here   Ma   You think that's right Ma

HANGING FROM THE TREE OF LIFE

Sometimes the heat gets to you   There is a danger to having a child live
My farthest neighbors   their only daughter   one day   disappeared
waiting for frost to dissolve on their skin in the early morning at a bus stop
Assumed taken by one of the other neighbors A thief who deals in bodies
The vast emptiness of a chaperone spirit   what is the point of your innocence
if it isn't where your body resides   She reappeared only
to be abandoned by her moving father   who in a sharp break decided
        to believe
he was an inadequate   removing presence   alleviating pressure
from the pedal & coasted   Her mother   his baby's mother   in a room
that smells like hauntings   she's put morphine in her mourning cup
A wailing body   a screeching heart   a slowed life she wants to be over

OASIS IN THE DESERT

I.
What are Pillars of the Community   The Chain Stores
They are attached to my collar The would be leash of glass
bottle Cokes & gummy worms swirled & knotted
dragging me in at 4am   to repeat eating snacks as meals
When my Mother saw where i was pulled to
every twilight she warned me
                                        they'll think you're trying to rob them

II.
This is all there is to consume
i'm closer to asleep than anything else
The fluorescents buzz   shaking the shelves
so the products move like their breathing
Either muscle memory or conditioning
i grab what i'm tied to

Self-checkout is closed so i am not alone
You   behind the register
Yes   you

are the only one left to talk to

Pleasantries are mixed into the air
i show you what i need
You tell me how much i owe

III.
i am breaking down into unoriginal pieces

i'm here every night sky morning

i can tell you your work schedule

i can't tell you why that matters to me

No longer a child
whose responsibility

am i
i ask *Am i alone*

In this twilight You need to keep your job
You need to keep lying You need me to leave

& i'll leave

Going home to a silenced house
adding whiskey to coke
Waiting until passing out turns to sleeping

HOSPICE LIVING

Before whatever is between the skin & bones disappears
before my Mom was my caregiver's skeleton   that couldn't leave
her bedroom i feed her i feed her me   i'm remembering i love her
i'm acting like it   i'm acting   though   i didn't expect to be
this person wiping skin fragile as papier-mâché   i can't hug you   you'd shatter
i can't feed you without feeding your killer   You are your senses & i am your shadow
responding to your bedridden beck & call
                                                                        let's stop clinging to definitions Please
broken apart   when I remember   what remains sicker in the dark
Let's go to a hospital   get talked into being ok
                                                      The cries are a wheezing sneeze
corked through a cough   hear her rupture

Brother
i didn't expect to be alive
long enough to be this person
She was supposed to bury me

Brother
Suicide has bribed me
i have spent a life fighting
back a wellspring of tears

This is that guilty love
          That your father is gone &
she needs you to bear that absence for her

i remember her i love her

so i'm caregiving wet smeared flesh
shouting out my brain & begging the Earth
let me hear the truth from its own tongue

WRITHING

Life It's all the same
that pill that saline that tube
you squeeze that thread going up your sleeve
in your collar in pain
Your bedroom & hell
crushing me into fine mist
it's all the same
Your eyes cataract glassy & the same
i say i love you
to make you to make me believe
you were worth any sacrifice i'll keep your body's
remains same in my bedroom & hell everything
feels the same

THE SPIRIT

GRAVESIDE MANNERS

My protector has passed into the glowing dark
Your grave is still
unmarked & i am waiting for your headstone
to be made & placed Today
on this graveside visit
i saw a beautiful Black youth
younger than me
pacing the cemetery
roads between the plots & endpoints
of hundreds of hearts broken further open
He was crying until he had to choose
between wailing or breathing He kept to his ache
kept pacing
i felt i should've said something   anything
but i was empty
i felt i should've given him the hug
i thought he needed to relieve one of us
but   like all the other ghost here   i witnessed

i often feel like a clay jug with a weakness
along its base My contents leaking out slow
& steady & no one has to tell me how it ends
i want to believe i was cracked
that this life's structural has had me

i am afraid i was born misshapen
unable to do the one thing i was made to

THE BLOOD CHAPTER

i'm becoming less thankful
each time we let the City push us
through this corpse's freeway veins
i'm in silence
watching humidity make skyscrapers tremble
to delay melting on our way home
My Brother drives me
hates me
We are linked like a vow
like things tethered to form blood
Moving through this flesh of time
we are stored like drawn blood
in Government housing vial trays
while this car
Mom's old car has become the centrifuge
for separating her children
Miles in here to & from hospital upkeep
for my Tylenol intake
nauseous hunched over
with the liver fully red
has strained us thin
like anticoagulants No *i'm sorry*

those were doctor words IV barbed in me with no commonness
& at this rate
i question if we will ever reform

FROM THE MAILBOX BEATRICE SPEAKS

Tú

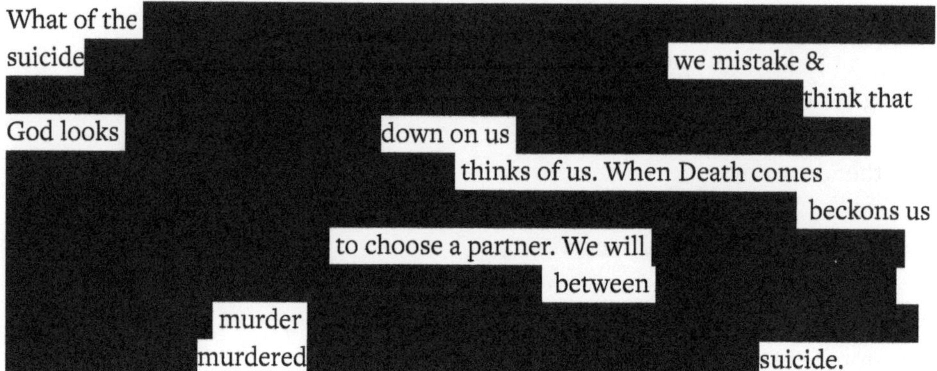

What of the
suicide we mistake &
think that
God looks down on us
thinks of us. When Death comes
beckons us
to choose a partner. We will
between
murder
murdered suicide.

Beatrice
Pvt.

UNTITLED LOVE POEM SHOPLIFTERS

My Brother's only advice

for love was Find a Queen

that steals & I have found you Take

my hand lead me & i'll walk in your footsteps

down the aisles My Best Man has block security's

line of sight with blackness Are you really gonna

support Capitalism Steal the marked up food

call me over when you're done

hug & kiss It's okay to make eating noises

on one another's cheek in public   nom yum nom

This will always go on too long for everyone

Love   i want to lie on the softest part of your thigh

Love   i want to know

which of your armpits stinks more than the other

You laugh

& that's all I ever wanted

The Police are called

i'll get carried away

away from you

You unsure with nowhere to go

The cardiac nothingness

The houseless heartache you realize

has always squatted within you after *I love you*

SACRIFICED TO THE GREATER GOOD

Beatrice's mom just got a flag in the mail

& an accompanying letter

more thanks than apology

i didn't go to the funeral

where

there was no body

The concession was made up
of the Undertaker's employees

Now their apartment smells
like the residue after chasing
the light at the end of the glass

soap bubbles on a hard white

rock Death vapors leak into the hall

The next month i saw her
tired with aging colors splinting
through the roots of her hair

This is the posthumous jab

STYX

Can you be going to Hell too soon
if you belong there   i'm waiting to form the horns out my skull i know
i have in my brain   Jesus be a gun When we die we all turn into stones
skipping across the water's surface
until we stop There's only one way the river flows   over us   i'm trying
to find the benefit to spending a life under the sun
The humidity is a stranglehold   Sweating until i get goosebumps
from the chills   & this wetness surrounds me
like i wasn't already baptized in hunger-filled pot bellies
& the purging of credit union accounts My neighbors wear a gut's gunshot
repair zipper wound like ancestral tattoos
                    in this circle Thank God
            there is nothing after this

VICES PHARMACEUTICAL REFILLS

It's too hot to have the window closed
from the ground Dante breaks into my open window

Aye nephew

aye nefhue
nephew what time
it is

You sure
it ain't 3
deliveries at 3 You sure
for your time Normally I'd ask
I promise
I'll pay fees n get food with this
ignored me
nefhue Aye at least we get this death
the pharmacist is good to us

Nephew thank you
aww bless you nefhue

You coulda
Thank you
til then

HOLLOWING POINTS

There are rules you learn in taking a charge
ankles' roots planted
forcing your turnover   scrap if you're losing

get the fade
if you can't get the W i got a jumper
off a heel turn a two to a three

shot into a drone clouded sky
with hope falling short
BRICK   A spectator & his car know

the importance of being loud
Who are you
to love me in a swish Walking over

Fucc up bench warmer
& who are you
for me to be a *FUCK BOY* in a miss

Taking L's has taught me torture
then how to feel
*On Blood   you dead**

He's reaching
pulling from under the passenger seat
Uncoordinated

            i can't react   i'll die   fuck it

or my brother   fuck
or some witnesses   waiting in sight
                             There's a bang
we know An empty police car is down
            the street   a posted hologram's

prying does not help me
My brother already gone
for his duffle bag   has taught me how
a pistol can split your face
when that niggas' blood ricocheted
off that bullet
& his sprinkles needled my pores
i feel it before i can describe it
cranberry custard mess All i see
is bleeding My right lid too sticky
to open My eye adhered & twitching
i try washing the pomegranate out
i occupy hours trying   splashing
saline city sanitation tap water
until the hot couldn't maintain
i tried weeping My eye twitches
like a body flailing   throwing a tantrum
desperate to convince breath to stay in
from the past All i see is bleeding *Why*
i should know Why Big brother
feature-less "I love you
I had to erase 'em." *i can't un-see him*
"Be or be done" i leak blood
"Forget it   It never happened"
fix your nature
What I saw "This never happened"
Nails as claws scratch out
memories dark & hard
a pencil without eraser is not a pen

you can't erase
only blight out

REPERCUSSIONS

At 4am in the shower i sing to forget
blood pumps out the body like summer waterparks

At 4am the police search for my brother in his room
        A concert
Let me see your see your hands. Hands HANDS
        The crowd makes demands of the performer

        *You don't know my whole story**
        i can't order my flesh to cooperate

Impatient firecrackers
        pyrotechnics

This song is for the boys that couldn't put it down
        deathened

        Officer i dream in all the spectrums of black

        Dear Black Officer what will you see
        when we appear in your dreams

LATTER DEGREE

The mattress is on fire
No forgotten cigarette's
to blame only me & my smoldering
My eyes boil then blister with
the image of my brother missing
the top enclosure of his skull
Brain matter is painted light
The coroner writes passages
none of them answer my questions
What walls keep us
safe & if they have collapsed
far enough is it possible to tell
what is breaking in or out
The fever's cured me
No longer drowning in mucus
vapors i can't find
the toilets water mouth
i'm throwing up the yellow vomit
scalding my molars If i reach out i'll melt
that flush knob If there is a river
i'd pray to be sunk with my family
The me holed by his bullet
my ribs liquify & skin recedes
into my pores i am leaking pus
like milk losing loose calcium
Looking down i see it falling
out of me like branches
looking down at their tapped tree
fevered   a glow
i am a light house
i am kindle
i've bonfire
black flames take the body
the light remains
the light is all that remains

VICES POVERTY

It's too hot to have the window closed
from the ground Dante breaks into my open window

negotiating with Virgil & an empty Pharmacy
Whose executions do you obey

Where you from
You in my shit talkin this
What are you to me
Where do you want to be put to sleep

Mutha fucca my yesterday is today
Have you ever seen the sun

The sound of his paltry limbs gun preparations
i close my window to give them privacy

AARON HERNANDEZ IS MY BROTHER

Dear Mom   i've lied
here since 2:30 a.m. Wednesday i don't need to
see the Super Bowl anymore
now i am the last child you have
          i don't know when it will be time to go outside again

between those 100 yards wrapped in air
that's a lighter fluid weighted blanket
In the Sun you can hit the temperature
where souls burn Coach is waiting to see
whom are flares & whom are stars Like my Brother
on our MLK corner for the neighborhood
where blood washes clean Through the in-zone
i see our church i'm trying to rep
for the neighborhood Coach on the sidelines speaks to me
Did you fumble or were you down? It's a turnover
no matter what How much blame do i want
i want all that is mine

HOME & THE HEART

Our floor is sticky with hot haunting   i can't drink the water
it tastes of pipes   the street is filled with the smell of hot meat
It is born & lingers   around the doorway & open windows
miner pickaxing through the walls
                                                                      In this circle there are no Dads
only the memories of them Before he faded from my life like thumping
from a passing car's speakers   unprompted   he told me about love
He said
Never move in with her   nigga   you'll end up homeless when she wakes up
& wants what she deserves   always   her to you
her to you
We are all trying to fight off what we've drank from a history of fear
Though   i keep drinking   i think i'm afraid to live
My brother said niggas are quick to use semen to cement union
out of fear that she'll be gone before you are
No concern about the shadows we leave in each other's lives
like anyone could bear to see how these shadows make their seeds grow
twisted   searching for a light   i miss him
Only four cried for Bro   No investigation   i heard they said
The monster deserved it
i don't know if he was that
                                                          but he is what i had

HEAT IS POSSIBILITY & SOMETIMES IT'S TOO HOT

Dear Brother
my flayed twin who walks with voids in his ceased lungs   i am like you
                We're all just tumbling in the open & we all agree not to notice & you
haven't heard from me since you died   i think   i want you to think
walking in crowds is more accurately thought of as moving through asteroid fields
                i know you like space   i hope that makes sense to you   i i
wouldn't be speaking to heat wave air if things were different but they ain't
Besides
this way our mother doesn't know this son is a fool who expects to sleep again

TRANSLATED FROM EMOTION

i haven't seen the sun
        just that there is light
i haven't seen a God
        just that there is
leaves of grass braided into rope
        i choke

Rest on eucalyptus leaves
Selfishness is the soul

&

my God is Suicide

Pour liquor on stone like witchcraft
Prophecies read on eucalyptus leaves
i'm too tired to believe there will be anything
        for me in the next season

red on eucalyptus leaves Dust
        A shadow cast by blood

WRITHING

Life It's all the same
that gun that gunpowder that casing
i squeeze that punctured upper torso
your collar in pain
Your bedroom & hell
sentence me to dream this memory
It's all the same
Your eyes choking bloodshot & the same
i say i love you
to make you to make me believe
is anything really worth the sacrifice i can't keep your body
the same in this bedroom & hell Everything
feels the same
i will meet you in that glowing dark Close my eyes
walk into the night leaving the door open
Embracing whomever may come

A Ghost Wearing A Dead Guy

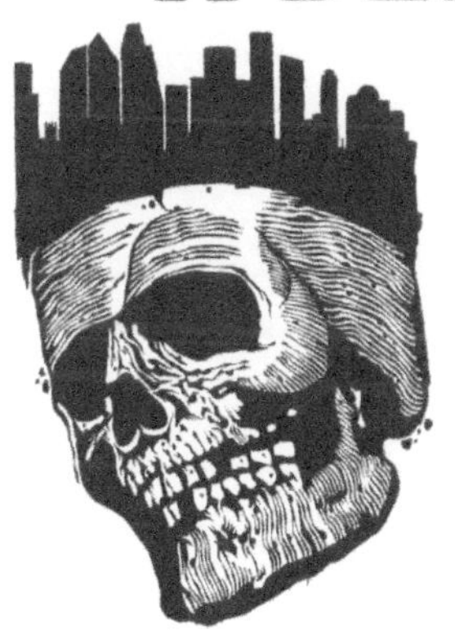

IF YOU'RE JUST WALKING IN & SEE THE WINDOW IT'S HARD TO TELL IF THAT'S OPPORTUNITY CLIMBING IN OR OUT

History often breaks down
into the question of who brought me
here & with that who   i can't remember
how i got here   just the blackness of life
leaving This room feels like watching paint
chips cracking There's a dryness
at the back of my throat The cracking paint
chips speak & i'm asked
"Do you know what you're interviewing for"
i do not care
what you have me do
Hanging behind a desk "You must
know I am the gallant mountain
swallowing calloused people
What you're interviewing for
is Suicide   To reek of derelict decay"
i watch them survey me
managing seer
the fluorescents burn silver
i'm waiting for absence
in the light "Take care of yourself
or you'll rot before your first day
at this Hearse Corporation"

MOURNING BORN FEET FIRST

All my memories are dreams
& her morning scent
lives on in our sheets
          My synapse snaps
from inhaling her cremation dust
A new anniversary amulet
dangling in her cleavage
causing her to break out
          like passion   breaching out
in radish hue   like her face
in our room
in those hours before waking alarms

          Clap off   lights out

          We always end up in the same position
& if out of our control
          Could you really do this forever

Hurricane postscript
rain finally tapering off
          hours ago
but the dropping
          of swooped up wildlife
          keeps the night noisy
For this weekday mourning breakfast
i got a graveyard on a plate
          a monument of our yard
i've got her saying my name
          it sounds like she's shearing me
into a man
          i would never choose to be
What of this appetite
Her face is disappointment
Placing the knife over the fork
i've probably left
the trashcan at the curb all night
again   my memories are dreams
          & i know nothing

IMPACT

The parking complex to the Hearse
Corporation lives at an intersection
Every day i walk into traffic
if you kill me kill me They speak
in honks   a *get the fuck out of my way*
in Morse code My sticky notes hang
around the computer like a funeral wreath
As coral yellow as the pinched bread
skin i feed the pigeons i know
when the day sets itself away
these man-made lights   these glaring desktop
screens have spoiled me
i don't need anyone to say
when it's gone you'll be blind
when it comes to darkness

WORK BEGINS AT MOLOCH'S   A HEARSE CORPORATION

Stapling papers   we're in perpetual layoffs   & always hiring
The plastic office plants withered
                                        Scrawled in finance sheets
                    Take What You Can
Business is bankrupt
                                agoraphobic & bankrupt

Through the swishing fluorescence's rain
painting us acid bleached silver
                                my love umbrellas out the elevator
                                    for another grind on me
Suicide feels her like I used to
        from the driveway   permeating inside

I'm pleading   *Go home*   *love*
Please leave   *what brought you*
here Leave   *no*   *please*
No thank you
She   wielding a crustless BLT hand   stabs at my face
I only eat you   *sweetheart* Distracting her

i move my hands
under a heavy-duty industrial paper cutter

Left or right? i ask
                    decisiveness of her

She presses her lips against my lobe
eyelashes catching uncombed hair & mouths

                                "You always make a mess"
This time I make a decision
        My right is the hand you've led me by
good-bye left

Laid off
        knifed out of responsibility
when the left hand path hits the cutting room floor

Sheared & my pieces pool

Appearing   behind her   with Socratic whispers

        Suicide introduces themselves

        with a truth The best demons know some

With sovereign palms   Suicide touches her heedless spine
                                        & whispers what sunrise does
                                        to a night of hopeful dreams

        she renounces him
but we could see that her pupils had become
well lit with dawn

        Bleached   on her way out the office
        she takes her time to confess to me
        "You used to be funny"

HTML

i'm working through lunch
searching through the archives
to learn how long ago
the last human died
The only thing these digital crypts
connect to is the same picture
of a little hand   no torso   barely an arm
too inexperienced to know
it's only depressing us by reaching out
like anyone will reach back
into a censored mass grave
of bodies blurred faceless

YES THIS TOO IS SUICIDE

Tell me pushpin cubical tapestry
who do I work for
until my hand rots
into carpal tunnel
Tell me about my Mom
& how i still live with her
How she still lives within me
while we're packed like gunpowder
in a suicidal chamber praying
for a City's finger
a S.W.A.T. team's pulled back hammer
to say it's time to be done

SAFETY CHEMS

Through the whiskey lining my coffee mug
i am drinking to retire
my liver   making use of my insurance plan
i can get a new one on layaway   i'm trying
to restart What is after drunk has been drank through
like diffusing
enough to kill   what can be in stomach acid
without charcoal   without safety
chems   without my vomit My Manager drops off more
coffee   taps my monitor & says *Keep up the good work*
through teeth they've grinded
impalpable   past stumps to the roots
How dangerous   to leave unprotected
                                        a tongue that's not covered
in insurance claims   76 proof drips down
from my lips to chin   i'm aiming to give a *Thanks*
          i'm doin' my best
          Trying & trying i'll always end up
telling the same story
using lies to keep it fresh

WHAT DID YOU DO AT WORK TODAY

My allergies love asbestos
My weeps short circuited
the keyboard spreadsheet sea
Sunken & swollen before the shore
a number pads made i am sneezing
waves & undertow A little
electricity & bacteria & i have Frankensteined
life at work i am sorry
i am watching them struggle
struggle without understanding

1ST & 15TH

This tie has infused into my sternum
as a cloth skin graft My co-workers
catch me saying i hate myself in the restroom
to their inconvenience We're all hiding
in dim lit stalls & ignoring that the office lights' leak
a fakeness through our clothes   into bone hollows
i am poisoned & i want to be poisoned
i have been trying to know how to open an artery
against security's crooked door handle
& make it look like an accident
& make it workers' comp

PYRAMID SCHEME

i am sorry
i can't find the best place to work
myself out
My Supervisor's again asking
for my body's overtime
There's no need to request
for this spirit   they have that already
i haven't been paid since i started
The Supervisor's clipboard has a glossy coffin
lead paint shine The paper is fingerprint skin wax
impressionable   shellacked
it's what we've all touched
i don't have proof
          my emails have been read
The Accountants are busy moving numbers
to make sense of what shouldn't be
i am being promoted
to Manager's Director Assistant to Chief's Druids Editorial Admin
There's sugarcane next to the coffee grounds
honey i will make the same i still haven't been paid
How many are like me My oldest new boss whispers
"Be grateful nigger   I am offering you this"

THE ABSURDITY   AN EQUAL IN SOCIETY

This morning headline reads
Blacks Diagnosed with Mass Hysteria
My coworkers nod
& sip from their morning mugs
i get up to share space with the only other blackness
in the break room The coffee
An uprooted & picked bean
Grinded & burned until it's useful
Often bleached with whiteness to be more palatable
i think of milk i think of sugar
i panic The sugar is white
& it doesn't visibly disrupt the blackness
i want to grab my coworkers   as if i could
to adorn them into this blackness
Darker than the clotting blown out the nostril

In the breakroom
i'm once again brought to my knees

Dear God   i know we don't talk
but fuck
i need anything other than what is

There is a silence so deep
i can hear the moon's humming

Why did i hope for any different

My coworkers walk in & speak of Indigenous curses
One says the next headline will be

Cannibalism on the rise
Are Native American Wendigos To Blame

The soup kitchen doors have locks on them
& food pantries are barren They say
the City has been abducting Native Americans
for interrogation needing answers
for its homeless turned wendigo problem

Who they expect savagery from

Me in this job that i hate that i need
Life if it's more than what you can't stand to grasp
then birds are my favorite artist
Building nest out of anything
even the dead Even though
corpses still move
& i've never felt bad for food before

From the ground i ask
Why are you so certain?

Who else could be responsible for this savagery?
One says
& we look into each other's eyes

TAKE IT UP WITH TAYA

i know those crumpled beer cans
should be described as half-buried
but
i see them as peeking
from beneath the soil like carrot tops
i watered them   with the last bits of backwashed tequila
that my mind in the hopes of preserving organs
or dignity   wouldn't let me finish
Something has to be brewing down there

i'm with you   propped between our cans
& the husky blue bottle that rolled free
to a stop from a metallic tabletop
that's molded with an old playground
fence's chain link pattern
It had been made a vase for your plastic roses
now replanted with footprints into this bar's dust yard
In this City these are our gardens

& we breathe in their air laced with cigarette aromas
i'm strangled with weak lungs
Hugs are a fragile goodbye
&   i'm hoping
ours pulls some wanting out of me   pushes
some wanting into you   i have snow thick tobacco cinders
on me   ashed   drifting onto you   This could be pollination

Another day where a fragment has us lied
against each other   Once a week now
drinking night   i have forgotten speech
& i only manage to accomplish this

& here is where reality seeps in
like a fifth of 140 proof spilt
into my fish bowl & my gills don't know

how to negotiate
i'm trying to negotiate
extend tape over my cracks
What if i noticed my loneliness
would never let her imposed seraphim wings molt

Then
Then what

Then i'll make it last a month
then struggle for some weeks
& then

i'm shaky holding shards that i've tried to make fit
i'm hoping she or someone with pity
will clasp my hands offer to stabilize
tell me i don't have to try so hard Please don't
uproot us from my daydream The little pile of burnt
white buds you tried to deposit
but the Earth wouldn't take
are now a compost heap i think i'm living for this garden

our garden embraced amongst all these contributions
to the world My stomach nervous moans
while my feet try to keep me vertical

i'm still craving
prolonged portions of this
before you squirm & say

You can let go now

THE BLOOD & WATER CHAPTER

"There's a no swim in effect" —*The City*

Hours since our designated lunch break
should've ended we let our bodies' lie
at the beach   i stepped toward the salt & water

because the City doesn't own the darkness of the sea

or the darkness of the crude it's layered with

                                        What is this Jellyfish fed petro
swollen on the shore   underbelly tentacles

free of electric life with black plague hickeys
peering through its cosmic torso

Brined & labored bitter
like how i imagined low hanging purpled fruit
to be poisonous as a child & how i imagine graying
meat now The Moon's respirator dependent paleness
sinks in into oil rainbow reflections How black tar kills

the vein   what is the Market Price of life
Overboard & desperate to float
kicking & pumping like a million
suicide freed Black captives Kicking & pumping
like a million breach freed crude gallons into aquatic life

The waves have changed
full of oil & sailing coffins

Death is natural
but not all deaths are

The filth water is as much water as everything else
                    indiscriminate
                    in its wrapping around
                    black polyping mounds
across the brown grains

Here comes the foam after the tidal wave dilapidates
Submerging my sandcastle & moving into my diabetic socks

    Yes
the only light I've known are those high-rise neons
that the skies aren't all tamed by

    & the clouds are stuttering
    with dry mouth   trying to salivate through grumbles

Taya is beached on the shore   dry in degrading company
The grains are harsh against her legs & back
i'm uncomfortable   unabsorbed like she is

like blackness would find a way
    The sand feels
    like it's hunting me
    over that refinery ointment

Like squids   jellyfish now piss ink Gulf water
i am careful speaking
here A open mouth will be

met with a gust & retribution
Jellyfish in hand Taya says *We are all killers*
Disgusted on our way out the primordial placenta

We never call home
& no one knows this but if you had just tried
you'd know how these waters strip your flesh scarlet

The clouds   done with us

done idling with threats lets loose
lightning sit down to watch us from offshore

i have never seen so clearly
than through the brightness of a kindled oceanic oil field
i have never seen something so on fire

SATAN IS A TITLE

Satan is a title like Boss
        You rarely see who rules
your life up close How many bodies
        are in between you From your cubicle
Ask the high rises how the balconies get bigger
        the higher you go Do not lean against the rails
you cannot trust them   they are there only for show

Ask the mailroom how it feels
to be crushed by words Performance evaluations
& severances erupting from the room
                                through the halls   Crushed by words

at the highest level
                at the basement
                                at this Hells exit & entrance

i saw a blonde cow feeding a black goat
i say *Be easy*
        the cow bites through my skin
        to the cream bone & licks my wound
i learned words & other poetries

aren't as strong as blood magic

Your lyrics aren't as strong as blood magic

Your allies will fail you
Your coworkers will see your torso as a shield

Seated
        but
        after desperately asked to un-recline

they'll ask is anything worth the sacrifice
They'll ask themselves is anything worth this sacrifice
They'll ask themselves if anything is worth my sacrifice

These are workplace mythologies
made from whispers Like who eats lunch alone
in the restroom stalls

Who'll really be promoted

Oh I've failed you & it is a race
to fire me before i quit This too is suicide

Satan is a title
like Mother How could you refuse
the next treatment

Who could blame you not taking this new pill
Yes   this too is suicide
Dignified   How will I know

if I'm making the wrong decisions Now
you've left me to dream alone

i pulled our home phone out the wall
wires & crackling & static
i introduced them to the kitchen tile

Transforming it into parts & i snacked
on all the shards i could stomach

Teeth met plastic & what followed
is the expunging of whatever is left
inside of me   blood

acid

more blood   more acid

this magic
No Ma'am
it doesn't go down easy

Satan is a title like
Son i know what it is to feel
like a window shaken by sound My friends & family

whom depending on how stories truly end
i may never see again
visit me in my dreams

The leaves rust & fall
What if i told you the truth
i feel like i meet the Devil in every mirror

in every memory a daydream
rewound life of should'ves

i'm in the mirror checking my teeth
                    hoping for healing
i have been sharing a toothbrush with Suicide

Satan is a title
like Addict There is shit everywhere
            A pack of queue-less dogs leaving
behind starvation dark breadcrumbs
            to find their way back to nothing

The malice that hurts true is addicting

Even though it's 100 degrees
addicts don't get cheat days
Hell too is a melting pot & though
we are cooked
                         together the bottom burns faster

Satan is a title like
        he was dead yet
in the cracks on the faces
        of dropped watches I have found
a time & place where we both still exist

Dead love & the smell of tears
from a life incomplete In some variation of holy
planets glow & release light

& we bask
Together
we bask

BOTTLENECK

Hear it   the 747's whirling around this Downtown no fly zone
with all the passengers' hearts synchronized   ticking along with the carry-on bomb's
godhead countdown There is no place like Hell like home
like traffic like the honking reaching into itself   finding ways to be louder
while my ears cave-in   i drool blood mid crosswalk & cross-town traffic
advisories are made about me When that's all been crushed out until
my canals are more like exhausted wounds i can hear this wet sphere ache & sing

AVARICE

The day just lost me in hours
Lunch can't come quick enough
A work day as long as it takes
for me to get honest with myself
i eat everything i love For the sugar high
annealed glass shard glazed donuts
about the office i don't know
but i know i use to love those
more than life & that's just another wish
that i would know how am I better off dead

DRYING IN HUMIDITY

Think about the City How worshipping happens
on every corner You completely stop at
red lights & signs to give thanks & to think
of your neighbors The collection plates are Styrofoam cups
held by the only real monks in this world God
i am tired of broiling in the concrete oven God
i was tired of being beaten by pestle in the mortar
before this Tired i have stopped sleeping to stop dreaming

WORK ENDS

Why is it so fucking hard to be happy
in dreams

like every funeral i know

Life
    on the road i pass a sedan
dying on the highway shoulder
    with its hazards on   hood open A highway second
past that   twin tow trucks with matching caution signs
    in formation like one's dragged the other

Taya   standing on the overpass
        guardrails like a gymnast i pull over
idle behind her roll my window down
        thinking You were never any of that

        i'm not begging her to come down

            Don't you know the way you should be?
There's a silence before a blunt thud
            Wordless

Released

    A specter wavering from my passenger seat
waves   beckoning   wanting my attention
    asking *Why don't we have anywhere to go?*

SURTR'S PATH

Disease let me know what's hereditary i am
my Father Everyday flames swallowed more
of his flesh & his bones turned to kindle
Feeding Blossoming Hot in my own meat
with each crackle more of me is translated
into these expanding charcoal petals
with roots slinking through my veins
This smoldering a primordial illness
there even before i started looking
away from my Mom's eyes in kindergarten
i'm afraid she will know
i can tell her what it is to suffocate
These ebony flames can't be head patted out
In my latest state i've accepted it will cremate me
When my husk is found
i only ask you throw away my ash

My thoughts let me know
You are the new Fire King
Ignited Feeling like my neighbor's bitch
she Lucy didn't deserve that but
she by chance wandered into the street
during my incandescence i was drinking
lies in a water bottle Sweating gasoline i left
as much of her on my front end as in the street
My neighbor's only daughter grieved
She buried Lucy but kept her dish on display
like a death mask
It wasn't just my fault
i hold the bottle
That was to put the fire out
In my Mom's car wearing a wildfire
i want
to finally cinder out My smoke reads
You have made cinders of all their lives

SELF INTEREST

Hunched over my office keyboard
with a release form deadline
stapled between my spine columns

beware where you keep stress

i check the election & i scream
Which of you voted to bring back crucifixions

The office is hushed with a *Wait*
you didn't

Below us   in this Hearse Corporations' atrium
Tarsiers choose what we all have
Suicide   bashing skull against tree limb
after jumping from one branch with no attempt to grab another
on the way down from too high Suicide is everywhere
This world still demands blood

complacency or death
        When the bumps are heard
        in an emergency lane
        they smooth out the farther you go
from me i have found a chain-link fence barricade
to hold like a child   through a hole   like i'm there
on both sides & haven't left you

TIME & A HALF

i don't try to lie about not doing work
i am a Director Assistant to something
i am back on the City's website reading
how the City could be worse The crime
has gone up unemployment has gone
up but there is industry growth
Burglary is a product of job creators too
There's been a rise in cannibalism To be bled
when you're broken open as a fountain mouth
so you can flounder   float in you
might be natural i think of the cafeteria
the parasites migrating out the imported pasta
i'll carry that with me We are all hungry

SIGNING OFF

History often breaks down
into the questioning who brought me here
& with what   i can't remember

Across from my cubicle
                    James is deleting

On the day of his retirement he's tightening
        the noose tie knot connecting him
to the dropped ceiling tiles
        as is tradition Our ceiling like a coffin lid

embedded with hang nails & drippings
        from retired people at the end of their lassos
Everyone knows this is how you scratch your way out

When someone hangs it up we are all emailed
        "It will only make sense after you fall"
          by Suicide   Their email signatures
                              says

"Take care of yourself
or you'll rot before your last day
at this Hearse Corporation"

WRITHING

        Life   It's all the same
that bridge   that overpass   that height
crushed bone severing that thread in your sleeve
        up to your collar   in pain
My bedroom & hell
you've just made this harder on me
        it's all the same
Your eyes ruby   wet & the same
i say i love you
to make you   to make this harder on you
Nothing is worth everything   i'll keep your body's
remains   same   in my bedroom & hell   everything
        feels the same

I TRY TO CONVINCE YOU IT ALL AMOUNTS TO SOMETHING

There's a slideshow of plant life ashes This is the where we should care part of matchstick cremations of forest

i try other methods to keep my wet in but it all dries into plant life ashes & i am alone with my incoherence & chants i try to break melancholy with always turn nightmarish because reality seeps in & i've got to find ways to compensate

There's a slideshow of plant life ashes
Viki emails me *We appreciate you hiding your face*
during the company meeting i've wept through
i'm researching about how to craft
a livable fantasy for me but i can't build images with hope
i don't have

i've turned the copy machine into wet memorials
but reality gets hot everything dries up into its own ashes

NOTES

The title *City of Dis* is taken from Dante Alighieri's *Inferno*. The City of Dis is a city that encompasses the lower circles of Hell in the *Inferno*. Generally, those guilty of fraud and violence are kept there. The "violent" are those guilty of committing either violence towards others, violence towards themselves, or violence towards God.

"Hollowing Points" contains the phrase "*On Blood you dead*" This is a quote from Young Thug from the song Skyfall by Travis Scott and Young Thug

"Repercussions" has the line, "*You don't know my whole story*" inspired by a line in the song "That Was Therapeutic" by RMR

The section title "A Ghost Wearing A Dead Guy" is a phrase taken from the TV Show *Adventure Time*

"Take It Up With Taya" is inspired by Tony Feher's Exhibit "Take It Up With Tut"

ACKNOWLEDGMENTS

Grateful acknowledgment and many thanks to the editors of the following publications in which these poems, sometimes in earlier versions, first appeared or are forthcoming:

> *Electric Lit*: "That Was A Ghost Wearing A Dead Guy: If you're just walking in and see the window, it's hard- to tell if that's opportunity climbing in or out," "This is a Spirit Melting Its Container: The Last Degree," "This is a body: Hollowing Points"
>
> *Gulf Coast: A Journal of Literature & Fine Arts*: "Sunflowers"
>
> *Indiana Review*: "Untitled Love Poem/ Shoplifters"
>
> *Midtown: A Journal of Writing and Fine Arts*: "Take it up with Leah"
>
> *Nomadic Ground/ Nomadic Press*: "Mourning Born Feet First"
>
> *Oversound Poetry*: "Surveillance"
>
> *Poet Tree*: "Graveside Manners"
>
> *Southern Indiana Review*: "Styx", "Safety Chems"

I am forever deeply indebted to my mom, Veronica Tyrone, for all her sacrifices. Thank you for not giving up on me. I also want to thank my family for their support.

I want to thank Dr. Beth Loeffreda, you saved my life. And thank you to Dr. Martha Serpas, you took a chance on me and paid for my first MFA application; without you none of this would be possible.

To my brothers: Matt Simpson, Arturo Soriano, Rhett Saludares, Jose Martinez, and Roger Ramirez, I love and appreciate you.

Thank you to my agent Adrian Shirk for helping me through all the uncertainty.

Thank you to all my mentors over the years who helped shape this book through compassion and understanding. Special thanks to Bhanu Kapil (you came when I needed you), Beth Loffreda, H. L. Hix, Martha Serpas, A Rattawut Lapcharoensap, Ed Skoog, Natalie

Diaz, Roger Reeves, Cornelius Eady, Rebecca Wadlinger, Karyna McGlynn, David Romtvedt, Adrienne Perry, Martin Rock, Jeffery Lockwood, Zachary Martin, Ian Stansel, Laura Eve Engel, Samuel Amadon, Liz Countryman, Glenn Shaheen, David Tomas Martinez, Aracelis Girmay, Danielle Pafunda, Andy Fitch, Mat Johnson, and Connor Bracken.

Thank you to both the Idyllwild Arts Summer Workshop and the Tin House Summer Workshop for giving me the tools I needed to complete this work. Thank you to the Matthew Shepard Social Justice Endowment and the Social Justice Research Center Endowment for helping fund my summer research.

Thank you to all my University of Wyoming MFA cohort and faculty for giving me the time and space to create. Special thanks to Elijah Johnson, Khalym Burke-Thomas, Korie Johnson, Sofi Thanhauser, Kristine Sloan, Auesta Safi, Olivia Wall, Carly Fraysier, LuLing Osofsky, Ammon Medina, Jess White, and Nick Mangigian.

Thank you to my dear friends and writers across the world. Thank you K. Iver, Nina Rašović, Leah Shlachter, Marissa Johnson-Valenzuela, Lindsay Willemain, Alicia Mountain, Luke/Luca Graham, Greg Montalbano, Grant D. Lewis, Sophia McInnis, Jen Jones, Tobias Johnson, and Alonzo Woods.

A deep thank you to my writing collective "Niggas with Profundities"/ "Niggas Writing Together" (name vote pending) members Dr. Joy Priest, Joshua Burton, Daniel B. Summerhill, Dr. Saddiq Dzukogi, and Bernardo Wade. You all have given me hope.

Thank you to my Houston writing community. Thank you to all of those both in and outside of the University of Houston. Thank you: Anthony Sutton, Anna Mebel, Aliah Lavonne Tigh (years of gratitude for you), Kaitlin Rizzo, Reese Lopez, Erik. B Brown, Catherine Niu, El Williams III, Amanda Ortiz, Shaina Frazier, Joseph Roberston, Chankrisna Tea, KT Herr, Maha Abdelwahab, Amanda Scott, Camila Cossio, Ramelle Ramos, Zarlasht Niaz, Stalina Villarreal, and Lau Eglin. And thank you to all members of the "Writers That Aren't Writing" collective for being there when I thought I was alone in the dark. And thank you Chelsea Rouen and Sherri Burrows for their many years of support.

Thank you to all my guiding lights in this book publishing process. Thank you, TRP, for taking a chance on me. I want to give a special thank you to both J. Bruce Fuller and Charlie Tobin for believing in me and for their unending patience. Thank you to Anthony Gassnola and FYHA Clothing Co. for letting me use their wonderful image for the cover.

ABOUT THE AUTHOR

RANDALL JAMES TYRONE holds an MFA from the University of Wyoming. He resides in Houston, Texas. His poems have appeared in Electric Literature's *Okey-Panky*, *Oversound Poetry*, and *Nomadic Press*. He has been anthologized in the *Bodies Built For A Game Anthology* by *Prairie Schooner*. He has received a scholarship to attend the *Tin House* Summer Workshop and was awarded the Bentley-Buckman Poetry Fellowship to attend the Writers Week at the Idyllwild Arts Foundation. He was a finalist for the *Indiana Review*'s ½ K Prize and a finalist for The X. J. Kennedy Poetry Prize. He's very excited for you.